Exploring
CAMBRIDGE
by
Rachel Riley

Copyright © 2018 Rachel Riley

The moral right of the author has been asserted.

Apart from any fair dealing for the purposes of research or private study, or criticism or review, as permitted under the Copyright, Designs and Patents Act 1988, this publication may only be reproduced, stored or transmitted, in any form or by any means, with the prior permission in writing of the publishers, or in the case of reprographic reproduction in accordance with the terms of licences issued by the Copyright Licensing Agency. Enquiries concerning reproduction outside those terms should be sent to the publishers.

Matador
9 Priory Business Park,
Wistow Road, Kibworth Beauchamp,
Leicestershire. LE8 0RX
Tel: 0116 279 2299
Email: books@troubador.co.uk
Web: www.troubador.co.uk/matador
Twitter: @matadorbooks

ISBN 978 1788034 579

British Library Cataloguing in Publication Data.
A catalogue record for this book is available from the British Library.

Printed and bound in Malta by Gutenberg Press Ltd
Typeset in 12pt Calibri by Troubador Publishing Ltd, Leicester, UK

Matador is an imprint of Troubador Publishing Ltd

For Elin, my champion.

Special thanks to Claire Hewson.

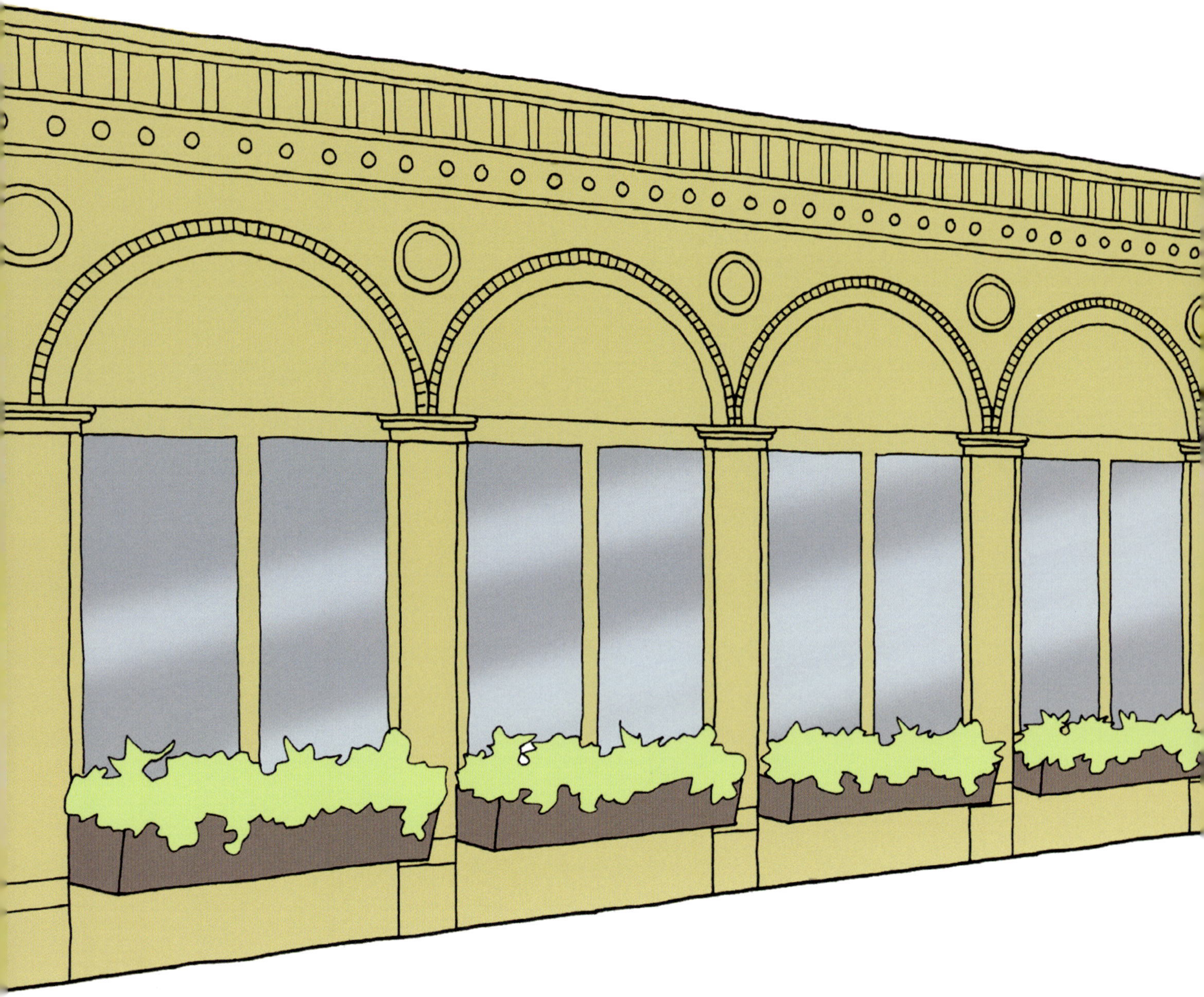

It's the summer holiday and we're having a weekend exploring Cambridge. I want to see the Boat Race, but Dad says it's the wrong time of year – and that it's held in London anyway.

Gran says that Cambridge is best known for its ancient university, which is one of the best in the world. She says that Cambridge is teeming with boffins and that some amazing scientific discoveries have been made in things like:

I think they're hoping some cleverness will rub off on me.

There are loads of things to do and we've only got a few days, so we'd better get on. The trouble is, we can't agree on which is the best way to explore!

"A bike!" says Dad. "That is the ONLY way to explore Cambridge. The city is almost flat so it's perfect for cycling. Look! There are bikes everywhere. Here is a special map that shows where the cycle paths are. Are there any bikes without baskets though?"

We start on Trinity Street at the Great Gate to Trinity College. There's an apple tree that grew from a cutting from Isaac Newton's apple tree - you know the one; where the apple fell on his head and gave him ideas about gravity? It was while at Trinity College that Isaac Newton worked on his theory about gravity pulling the Moon to the Earth and the Earth to the Sun.

We find the tree and take a photograph.

Q1: At the Great Gate to Trinity College is a statue of its founder, King Henry VIII. What unusual object is he holding in his right hand?

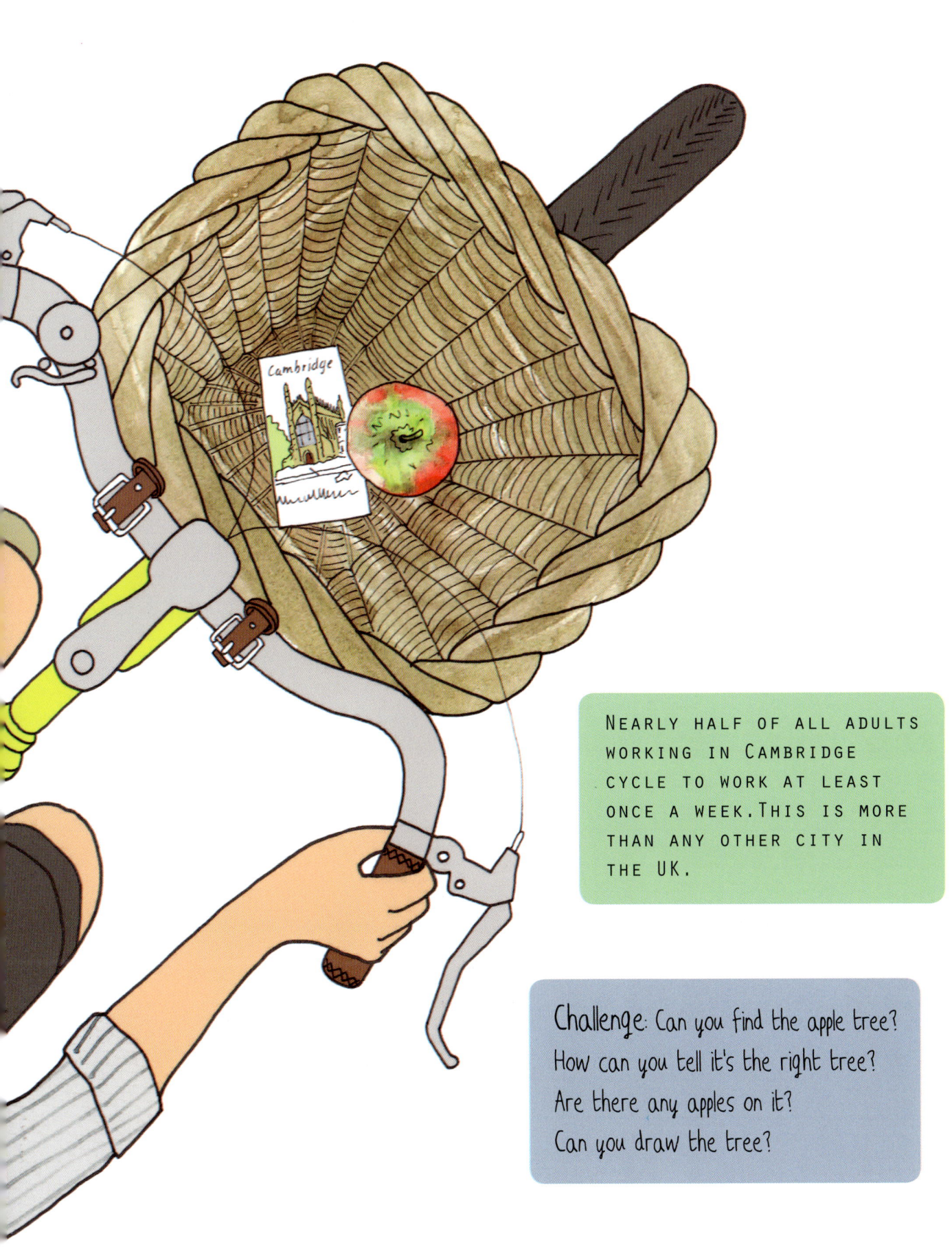

Nearly half of all adults working in Cambridge cycle to work at least once a week. This is more than any other city in the UK.

Challenge: Can you find the apple tree?
How can you tell it's the right tree?
Are there any apples on it?
Can you draw the tree?

Q2: What creature is perched on top of the Corpus Clock?

We weave through windy streets looking at beautiful college buildings and peer through iron gates into pristine courtyards. We pedal along King's Parade and stop at the golden clock. Look, it's about to strike the hour!

Challenge: On the corner of Benet Street and Trumpington Street is the Corpus Clock - a magnificent golden timepiece. Can you work out how to tell the time?

We pick up speed and whizz across parks and commons, stopping at Parker's Piece for ice cream. Mmmmmm double mint choc chip, my favourite! Next we have a game of cricket. It's Mum and me versus Dad and Gran. Gran turns out to be an excellent bowler! Who knew? Cumberland keeps running off with the ball, so we call it a day and get back on our bikes.

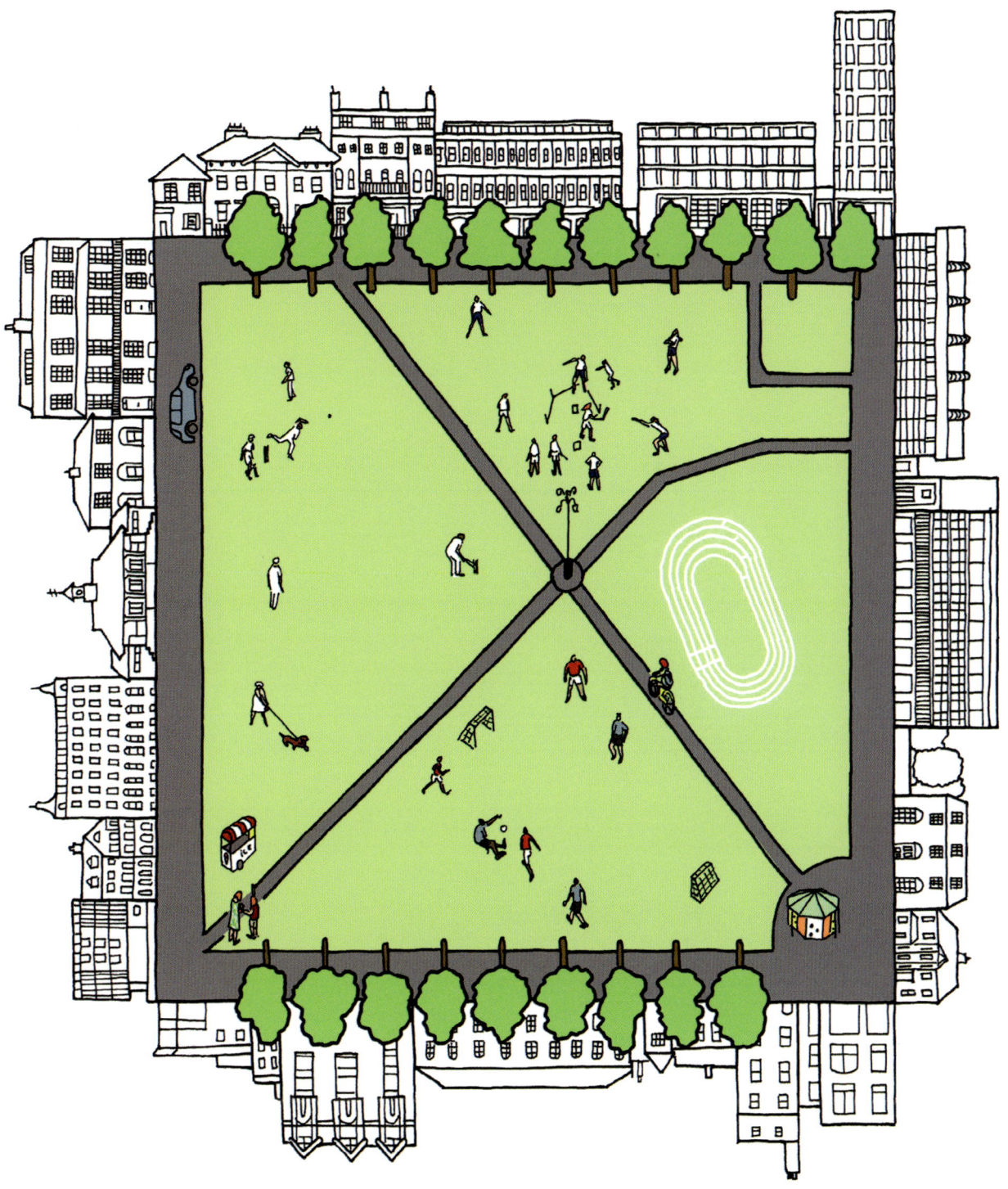

It is said that the modern game of football started on Parker's Piece. The 'Cambridge Rules' were drawn up at the University of Cambridge and were first played here in 1848. They heavily influenced the creation of the Football Association's rules on which today's game is based.

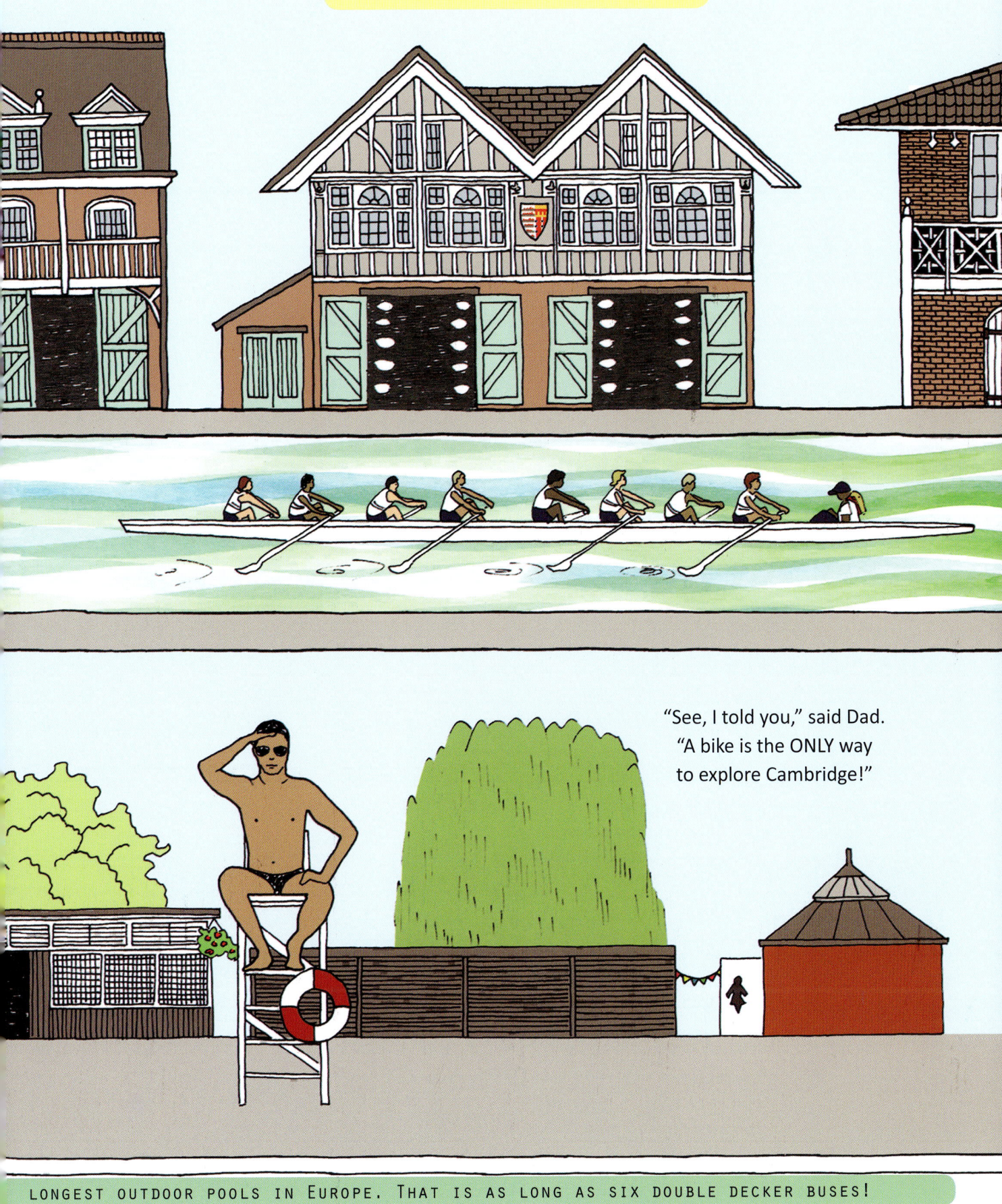

"What I would like," says Mum inhaling deeply, "Is a ride on a punt. We can sit back, relax and watch the world go by. Let's eat strawberries and cream and lie back in the sunshine. Apparently the best views of Cambridge are from the river."

The punt takes us along the backs of the colleges, past King's College where the famous choir sing. We pass under majestic bridges with weeping willows cascading into the water. Mum is in her element. The bridges are all very different and the punt can only just fit under some of them. Our punt chauffeur is a student in Cambridge. She expertly steers using the long pole and we manage to avoid collisions, unlike some other punts!

Until the 17th century, big sea ships sailed into Cambridge, which had a wealthy inland port. Then in the 17th century, the fens to the north of Cambridge were drained and the river became too shallow for large ships to reach Cambridge.

Q4: Whose head is famously buried in the grounds of Sidney Sussex College?

Challenge: Draw your favourite bridge. Why do you like it? How does it stay up?

The chauffeur tells us funny stories of pranks that Cambridge students have played. Clever students do clever tricks! Here are some:

Clare Bridge, the oldest bridge in Cambridge, has large stone balls along its parapet. One of the balls had been taken away for repair. Students made a replacement ball from paper mache and put their fake ball where the missing ball had been. As a punt of tourists approached, the students began to push their ball off the side of the bridge, heaving and straining as if it were a mighty weight. Fearing for their lives, the tourists leapt overboard, only to see the lightweight ball bobbing up and down gently in the water.

THE BRIDGE OF SIGHS IS PART OF ST JOHN'S COLLEGE AND WAS NAMED AFTER THE BRIDGE OF SIGHS IN VENICE. IT BEARS LITTLE RESEMBLANCE TO THE ONE IN VENICE, EXCEPT THAT THEY ARE BOTH COVERED OVER.

Q5: How many stone balls are on the parapet of Clare Bridge?

Another time, in the dead of night, some engineering students managed to heave a van onto the roof of Senate House. This is a very important building where university degree ceremonies are held. They hoisted it up using ropes and pulleys. The police, fire brigade and civil defence all tried but failed to lower it down off the roof. In the end it had to be cut into tiny pieces! How they did this without a single person noticing remained a mystery for fifty years.

Challenge: Can you make a mini hoist using rope and two rock climbing hooks (carabiners)? You will need to hang it from something like a ladder placed horizontally across two trestles. Can you make the load easier to lift by adding a third hook?

We are feeling adventurous so we hire our own punt and head away from the city towards the pretty village of Grantchester. Dad does most of the punting but I have a go as well to show him how it's done.

We tie the punt and walk up the grassy meadow to The Orchard. Famous people like Alan Turing (who invented the computer), Ernest Rutherford (who split the atom) and A.A. Milne (who wrote Winnie-the-Pooh) have taken tea in the gardens. Even HRH Prince Charles has enjoyed a slice of Victoria sponge under the apple trees!

The person who is most associated with Grantchester is the Georgian poet Rupert Brooke, who wrote the well-known poem 'The Old Vicarage, Grantchester'. The last few lines are about some happy times he spent here:

'Stands the church clock at ten-to-three
And is there honey still for tea?'

THE VILLAGE OF GRANTCHESTER IS SAID TO HAVE THE HIGHEST CONCENTRATION OF NOBEL PRIZE WINNERS IN THE WORLD!

We have enormous scones with jam, then punt back into the city. Dad takes Cumberland to the hotel and Mum, Gran and I go to Downing College to see an outdoor performance of Shakespeare's 'A Midsummer Night's Dream'. We enter through some big gates, lay our blankets on the lawn and spread out our picnic. The lawn is enclosed by stately buildings, which appear to glow in the setting sun. I find the play a bit tricky to understand, but I get the idea. There are funny lines like:

'O me, you juggler, you canker-blossom, you thief of love!'

Mum is entranced. "This is the life," she says and smiles, sipping her drink. She glances up as a drop of rain splashes on her nose. Did anyone bring an umbrella?

Challenge: Can you try punting with the pole? Can you steer the punt in different directions?

Q6: The University of Cambridge is made up of 31 different independent colleges. How many can you name?

It's a new day and Gran and I decide that we would like to go on the open-top bus. It will be fun to sit on the top deck and see everything from up high. Gran says she'll be glad of a rest after yesterday's exertions. We sit upstairs and enjoy a bird's-eye view.

Stop 2. Ding! We hop off at the University Museum of Zoology. There's a HUGE whale skeleton, 21 metres long, hanging from the ceiling. There are specimens of rocks, fossils and animals collected 185 years ago by Charles Darwin. It's fascinating to think that these objects helped our understanding of where human beings come from. Over the road is the Sedgwick Museum of Earth Sciences. There are dinosaur fossils that are MILLIONS of years old. There are the remains of hippos, lions and MAMMOTHS that were all discovered in Cambridge. They roamed the area 120,000 years ago when Cambridge was as warm as the grasslands of Africa...

CHARLES DARWIN WAS A NATURALIST WHO IS KNOWN FOR HIS THEORY OF EVOLUTION. HE COLLECTED MANY SPECIMENS WHILST ON A ROUND-THE-WORLD VOYAGE ABOARD HMS BEAGLE.

IN THE FITZWILLIAM MUSEUM, SOME OF THE EGYPTIAN OBJECTS ARE OVER 6,000 YEARS OLD!

The bus stops at an imposing museum called the Fitzwilliam. It is packed with treasures, from weapons and armour to great masterpieces by Renoir and Picasso. There is even a mummified cat from ancient Egypt! I pick up a trail pack from the information desk that takes me through the Egyptian galleries. I am an explorer in Ancient Egypt, finding clues and drawing important objects. I learn about pharaohs; why and how they were turned into mummies. Gruesome!

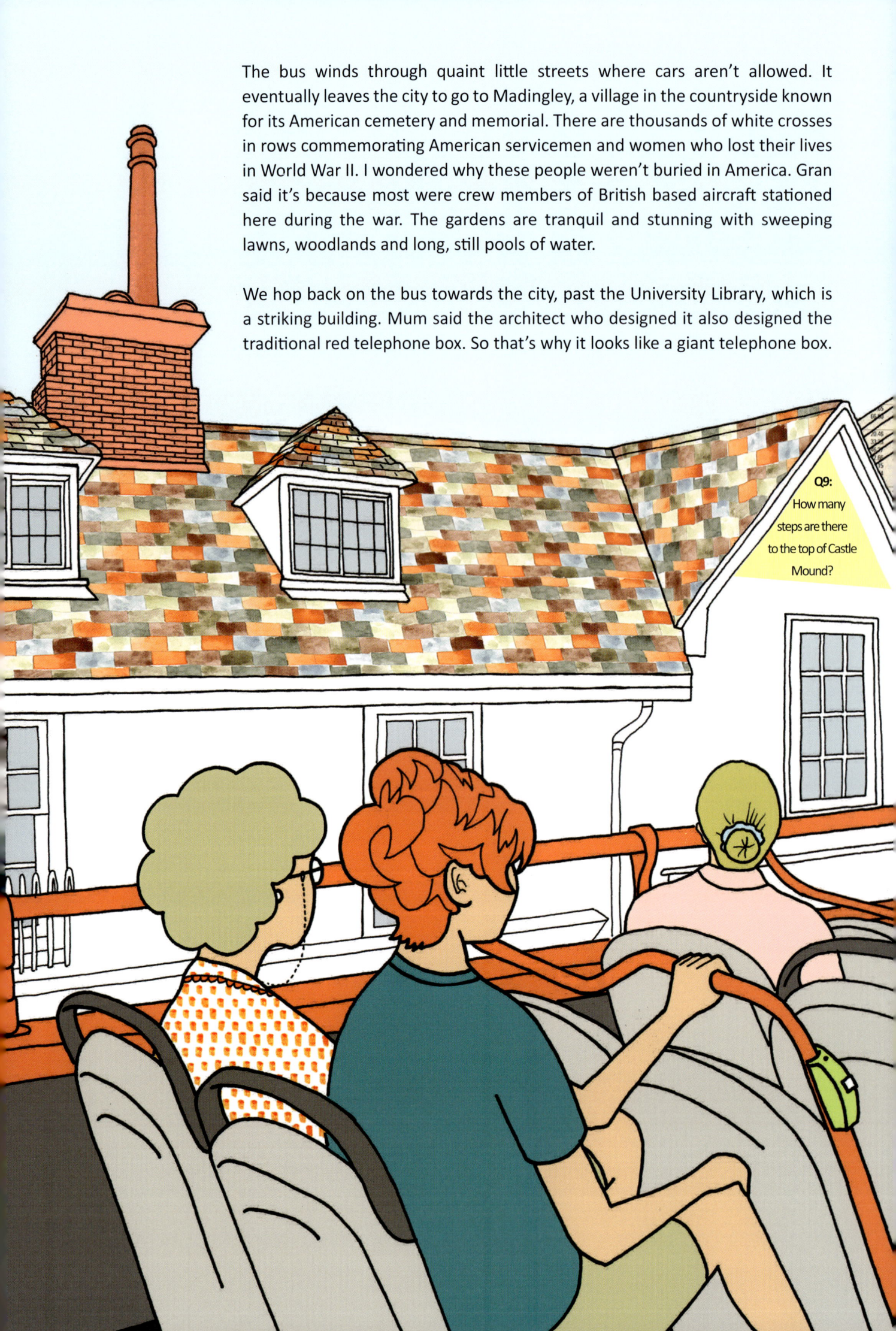

The bus winds through quaint little streets where cars aren't allowed. It eventually leaves the city to go to Madingley, a village in the countryside known for its American cemetery and memorial. There are thousands of white crosses in rows commemorating American servicemen and women who lost their lives in World War II. I wondered why these people weren't buried in America. Gran said it's because most were crew members of British based aircraft stationed here during the war. The gardens are tranquil and stunning with sweeping lawns, woodlands and long, still pools of water.

We hop back on the bus towards the city, past the University Library, which is a striking building. Mum said the architect who designed it also designed the traditional red telephone box. So that's why it looks like a giant telephone box.

Q9: How many steps are there to the top of Castle Mound?

It's quite late now, so we have fish and chips - hooray! Dad wants to see the sunset from Castle Mound, the highest point in the city. Buses have stopped for the day so we walk there. It's not far. I can't wait to see the castle. I love castles. It's starting to get dark when we arrive, but we climb the steps to the top of the mound. Hang on, where is the castle? The view is awesome and the twinkly lights of Cambridge look magical. What a fantastic weekend!

There is no castle on Castle Mound! Cambridge used to have a castle, which was built by William the Conqueror in the 11th century. Cambridge was an important strategic point between London and York. The only remaining part is the motte (a big mound on which a keep would have been built). The motte is 10 metres tall and rests on the highest point in the city. Some stone from the castle was used to build the University.

Challenge: Climb to the top of Castle Mound and take a photo of yourself on the summit.

We had a brilliant time in Cambridge, exploring by bicycle, punt and open-top bus. In the end I couldn't say which was the best.

If you decide to explore Cambridge, I hope you have as much fun as we did!

We didn't have time to visit all the places we would have liked on our whistle-stop trip. Here's my wish list for next time.

The Museum of Cambridge

This is a museum about ordinary local people and how they lived in the past. There are little glass balls that people hung in their windows to deter witches from seeing into their homes, and lots of old things to try out and play with.

Fitzbillies

This is a cafe that is famous for its very sticky and very tasty Chelsea buns.

King's College Chapel

The grandest and some say most beautiful building in Cambridge with the largest fan vaulted ceiling in the world (it's not held up with columns). The Chapel has a spectacular history - it took over 100 years and the reign of five kings to complete. You can hear the choir sing Evensong most days.

Wren Library

The library of Trinity College and the largest of the Cambridge college libraries. It houses significant rare books and manuscripts, including A.A. Milne's Winnie-the-Pooh and a lock of Sir Isaac Newton's hair!

Scott Polar Research Institute

Here you can find out what it's like to travel to the Arctic and Antarctic and learn how to survive some of the most extreme conditions on Earth. The museum contains artefacts, photos, journals and clothing from the very first expeditions to the Polar Regions. Brrrrr!

Skate Park (Jesus Green)

There's an awesome skate park. Next time I will bring my board and do some flips and grinds.

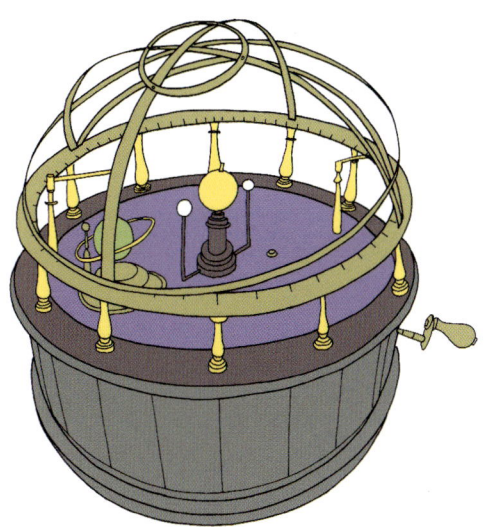 

Whipple Museum of the History of Science

This museum has scientific instruments and models from the Middle Ages onwards. There is an orrery (a moving model of the Earth, Moon and Sun) from 1750 showing the planets that were known at the time. There's no sign of Uranus or Neptune.

Museum of Archaeology and Anthropology

You can see artefacts from human history that help our understanding of how humans lived in the past. The oldest object is a 1.8 million-year-old stone tool from East Africa – and there are objects from Captain Cook's Pacific voyages too.